All rights reserved by Andrea Williams. This book or any portion thereof may not be reproduced or used in any manner whatsoever without the expressed written permission of the publisher except for the use of brief quotations in a book review.

ISBN: 978-0-578-31191-3
Distributed by Power Of Purpose Publishing
Www.PopPublishing.com
Atlanta, Ga. 30326

All rights owned and reserved by Andrea Williams

Contents

INTRODUCTION	1
SECTION I. REASONS PEOPLE COMMIT SUICIDE	6
SECTION II. MY STORY	12
SECTION III. THE POWER OF BEING FEARLESS OF THE INEVITABLE	16
SECTION IV. FAMILY/FRIENDS OF SUICIDE VICTIMS	26
SECTION V. RESOURCES FOR PROFESSIONAL HELP	35

Introduction

This book was written with anyone who has ever had suicidal ideation, or who has ever made a suicide attempt in mind, as well as anyone who has suffered through the pain of having to bury a loved one who has committed suicide. My intentions are to teach you how to save yourself by shifting your perspective on using death as a method to escape the pain that comes with life's disappointments. This book is intended to help someone help themselves by giving them the encouragement to commit to a life that makes them happy. Life is full of adversities. If you are not prepared, life can really knock you down and cause you to lose hope, but having a goal and a plan can help you overcome almost anything.

This is not a book that is going to encourage you with empty words of encouragement like: "keep your head up", or even worse for those who seriously want to die, "At Least you're still alive". If someone truly wants to die, being alive is *not* the best thing that could be going for them at that moment. Words of encouragement come from good intentions, but they usually do nothing to help us find actual solutions to our problems, nor do they help those who suffer from a strong desire to no longer exist in that moment.

According to the National Institute of Mental Health (NIMH), **suicide** is death caused by self-directed injurious behavior with intent to die as a result of the behavior. A **suicide attempt** is a non-fatal, self-directed, potentially injurious behavior with intent to die as a result of the behavior. A suicide attempt might not result in injury. Then there is **suicidal ideation** which is where one thinks about, considers, or plans to commit suicide, but never acts on it. According to the Centers for Disease Control and Prevention (CDC), in 2019, suicide was the tenth leading cause of death in America and claimed the lives of 47,500 people. That number does not include any undocumented deaths from suicide. In 2020-21, I know of several people who have committed suicide, which is why I wanted to write this book. I have been on both sides of the spectrum, as a person who has had suicidal ideation as well as someone who has lost loved ones from suicide.

Being someone who has suffered from depression, anxiety, and suicidal ideations since I was 8yrs old, I can honestly say that I can relate to those that feel like life is exhausting, and that death would give them the relief their body and soul needs. I know what it's like when you've lost your will to live and are numb to having any desires at all. Life can seem unfair and feel like one big setup for failure sometimes. Anyone who has experienced suicidal ideation has their own reasons as to why they feel the way that they feel regardless of what anyone on the outside looking in thinks. My goal is not to belittle your feelings, but to shift your perspective on using suicide to resolve any of your problems.

You see the good news is, ALL problems have solutions, and ALL problems are temporary, it's just a matter of how you perceive things and your level of patience. All problems have a solution, but self-inflicted death will never resolve any of them. Death isn't the end but the beginning of a new journey that none of us have ever experienced. There is no guarantee that death will mean you no longer exist, or that you will simply disappear and be at peace. Your problems will still exist, and someone else will have to deal with them, trying to process your death as well. It is best to let death occur naturally since it is inevitable anyway.

The good news for anyone considering suicide is that life is temporary because you are going to die one day anyway. Death is inevitable. There is nothing you need to do to make that happen. One day you will die, and it won't be scary for you because it will be unexpected, and it will be relieving because your spirit will be prepared and ready for the next part of its journey. Your life will *expire* on its intended date, and you will finally be at peace. Now if you die prematurely, by committing suicide, I can't say what will happen to your soul. As an overthinker, there were all types of "What Ifs" and epiphanies that I had during my suicidal ideations and attempts. I encourage you to let it all playout naturally, and find relief in knowing that your stay here on this planet is temporary, just like your current problems.

This book was written with the idea that I do not have a lot of time to make my point with a reader that may or may not be contemplating suicide. So this book will be short, sweet, and to the point. While you are reading this book you will be simultaneously creating a plan to recommit your life to living on your own terms. This plan will be a great reference for you when you need a reminder of your "Why" for living. As you recommit your life to doing the things you love with the ones you love, you will soon notice that life isn't as bad as you think, and you will hopefully shift your perspective on suicide.

I am not a professional mental health counselor, but I will guide you towards professional resources that I personally used in Section V of this book, that can help you re-discover a sense of self-worth through professional counseling if you feel that's what you need. I will share with you resources that I used to discover my purpose along my journey, and how I manifested a new job making great income and providing me with the flexibility I was looking for.

This book is broken down into five sections, and at the end of each section there will be questions that will help you re-direct ways you can pursue living a more fulfilled life, while doing all the things you love. There is space provided within the book for you to write down and express some of those things that you may have bottled up inside as well. In the first section, we will discuss the top 15 reasons why most people commit suicide, none of which are valid reasons for committing suicide, but are valid reasons for feeling sad and/or depressed.

Section I.
Reasons People Commit Suicide

For those who have never experienced having suicidal thoughts, consider yourself lucky. Battling depression, or losing your will to live is a horrible space to be in. Everyone says, "You should talk to someone", but sometimes there is no one to talk to that will understand. Sometimes the people you talk to only make it worse because they belittle a person's reasons for wanting to commit suicide in the first place; which can make a person feel like their feelings are not valid. The most common questions are, "How could someone do such a thing to themselves?", or "Why in the world would anyone ever want to kill themselves?" According to Mental Health Daily, these are the 15 most common causes for suicide:

- *Mental Illness
- Traumatic Experience
- Bullying
- Personality Disorders
- Drug Addiction/Substance Abuse
- Eating Disorders
- Unemployment
- Social Isolation/Loneliness
- Relationship Problems
- Genetics/Family History
- Philosophical Desire/Existential Crisis

- Terminal Illness
- Chronic Pain
- Financial Problems
- Prescription Drugs

Dealing with the disappointments of life is stressful and can make you want to give up on life entirely, especially when you have lost hope that things will ever get better. Most people will always look at the actions of others introspectively. They will say, "I can't think of anything that would ever make me want to kill myself", or "Wow, that was dramatic, I would have never killed *myself over that.*" The problem is, it isn't you, it's someone else who has to manage their own feelings and actions. You can't compare what you would do with someone who you are not because everyone responds to stress and depression differently. You will never understand how painful life is for some people. For some, it is an everyday struggle just to wake up and keep going.

As a person who has battled suicidal thoughts, there are a few things that have kept me going. One of them is *tenacity*. Tenacity by definition means the quality or fact of continuing to exist; persistence. At times when I no longer wanted to exist; I simply did nothing at all. The phrase *"peace be still",* is something I recite as a mantra to myself to dismantle these occasional temporary thoughts. Having dealt with thoughts of suicide for so long, I have learned that these thoughts come and go, and occasionally life does get progressively better. I think about all the times I wanted to commit suicide but didn't. I think about all the fun I've had in between those thoughts of fantasizing about death. Things I experienced and people that I met that I never would have met if I had killed myself when I wanted to.

No matter what you are going through, understand that it is temporary. Give up on the problem, but never give up on your life because your problems are temporary, but you are eternal. There are still some things that life has to offer you. There are some wins, some exciting and fun moments, new opportunities, new relationships; there is still more to experience. Death isn't anything you need to rush, because at any moment or at any time it could happen to you naturally. Tomorrow isn't promised. Try to find and develop new ways to enjoy the present moment with the ones you love.

Negative thoughts about the future cause anxiety, and living in the past causes depression. To avoid these feeling of anxiety and depression naturally without taking drugs or alcohol, do the following:

1. Try to quiet your mind and stop all thoughts. Envision your favorite color and focus on it to help clear your mind. By focusing on a color you will distract your thoughts that are causing you to feel suicidal.

2. Take deep inhales and long exhales. Breathing allows oxygen to flow to the brain and operate at a higher/clearer level. This also slows down your heart rate when you're feeling anxious.

3. Do this for 5 minutes minimum, but for as long as you would like. Allow yourself to receive any messages that arise. Don't try to think of any reasons or answers, just let it flow to you naturally. When I meditate during hard times, I like to repeat this as a mantra, "this too shall pass."

Understand that these thoughts of suicide no matter the problem you are facing is all temporary. Life is full of possibilities and miracles. This too shall pass.

Questions for Reader:

When was the last time you had suicidal thoughts?

_____

_____

_____

Have you ever attempted to commit suicide? If so, what did you try to do to yourself, and why?

_____

_____

_____

What problems do you have that you believe death will resolve?

_____

_____

_____

What do you think has been keeping you alive so far?

_____

_____

_____

Do you think there are any other solutions to your problems aside from death? If you answered yes, you are right and please list them. All you have to do is create an action plan on how to do it.

_____

_____

_____

If you answered no, I have something else to share with you in this book. Whether you answered yes (or) no please keep reading. In the next section I would like to be transparent, and share one of my first encounters with thoughts of suicide.

Section II.
My Story

I was only 8 years old when I first decided to speak up about having suicidal thoughts. I had been battling depression for years before I spoke up and told my grandmother about the thoughts I had been having. I grew up in Cleveland, OH with a mother who at that time was young, impatient, and in my opinion didn't really understand me as an individual. I would see my father most weekends, but my father had more of a relationship with my older brother because he could understand and relate to a boy more than a girl. My mother and father were divorced and tended to have fist fights whenever they did see each other. I was very sensitive to the volatile altercations which made me turn inward for protection of my feelings. As a child, I dealt with a lot of emotions by myself because I didn't feel my parents would understand if I spoke up and talked to them about it.

When I was 8 years old, I confided in my grandmother by asking her, "Do you think anyone would care if I died?" I asked her this question because at that age I felt like a burden to my parents and my brother; I felt like an outcast. My grandmother exclaimed, "Drea! Of course we would care if you died. I would be absolutely devastated if you died. Don't ever think like that! What made you ask me that?" I wasn't able to articulate why I felt I would be better off dead as a child, it was just a question I had and continued to have throughout my life. It was this feeling of *I don't belong*. I asked that my grandmother not tell anyone that I had been having those thoughts, but she told my mother anyway.

My mom called me downstairs, and I knew exactly why she was calling me. I was so afraid of my mom who was very authoritative and impatient. She said to me, "If you ever want to kill yourself, stand at the end of the driveway and I'll run you over and kill you myself." As shocking as that may sound to some, I was not shocked at all. That was my mom. That's how she was at that time. Stern and impatient for any non-sense. I was actually afraid to die, but I lived a life fascinated with the idea of death and that one day all of this would be over. While quietly battling depression and suicidal thoughts throughout my life I tried to seek solace from God. I asked Him many questions because life was very confusing to me, and it sometimes still is.

I highly recommend you ask God questions about any concerns you have regarding your life, and be receptive to the response He will give. God communicates with all of us differently. I can't tell you how He will respond, but ask the questions, and the response will come. You will know it's a response from God because it will be an answer you never would have thought of. It will be a response full of wisdom and knowledge greater than your own.

I am still here because I don't see the point in actually killing myself. Although I have a therapist I can talk to, I still lack the love and support where it is most needed, so sometimes life can be a bit challenging; especially when you feel alone and misunderstood. This is why I have such a soft spot for those who battle suicidal thoughts. I understand exactly why some go through with the act of suicide. I understand exactly what it feels like to be in a place of hopelessness, and what it feels like when you no longer have a desire to become or accomplish anything in life. For some, death is the one thing they can do successfully after feeling like a failure most of their life.

Knowing what I know now, I am not tempted by thoughts of suicide and they do not occur as frequently. I am still a work in progress, and I believe I will always be a work in progress. I still believe it to be my life's purpose to provide a support system for those who battle suicidal thoughts, especially from lack of love, support, or just feeling hopeless like life is not going to get any better. Those emotions always passed, and better ones replaced them eventually every time. In this next section, I am going to share an epiphany I had that is a better solution than suicide.

Questions:

What is your story? When did you first have thoughts of suicide?

_____

_____

_____

Section III.
The Power of Being Fearless of the Inevitable

Despite how anyone may feel by referring to people who have suicidal thoughts or who commit suicide as being *weak*, there is still a power one has once they reach the point of wanting to commit suicide that can be used for strength. It takes a lot of strength to go through life with depression and anxiety, and make it to this point. What it means to be fearless of the inevitable, is to be unafraid to die to receive a feeling of relief from whatever you are going through. Death is inevitable, and it is a fate that we will all have to go through at some point in our lives. If you are willing to die to feel relief, you should be willing to live because you have more control over your feelings and experiences alive than you do dead. Having a willingness to die can help you live life more courageously without fear of the outcome.

The desire to feel relief to the extent that you are willing to take your own life is unnecessary. You don't have to die to achieve a sense of peace, happiness, or just to end the suffering. All of those things are still achievable while alive. Since we don't know (for sure) what will happen to us when we die, who's to say that death will bring about peace, happiness, and end any suffering, especially if it's self-inflicted/or a premature death? What you should consider instead, is allowing an old/outdated version of yourself to die and rebirth a brand new version of yourself moving forward. You don't have to die to disappear. You can remove anyone or anything from your life to achieve that same sense of peace.

You can create the life you want right here, right now while you're alive. Just like plotting your death, you can plot your life. You could sell your belongings, quit your job, completely block out anyone, and prepare to live the life you want anywhere on earth with whomever you wish, if anyone at all. Live your life to the fullest, without fear. You see, if you kill yourself you'll never get to accomplish growing and developing into a greater version of yourself that you were meant to become afterall. All of us, no matter how old, are always growing, learning, and progressing. By being fearless of death, this can give you the power to live life uninhibited. So much of what we avoid doing in life that we believe will make us happy is avoided because of fear. I am telling you, you have a greater power within you if you are not afraid to die. A lot can be accomplished for your greater good without the fear of death.

You can silence the noise from others without killing yourself. If you die today, I honestly can't tell you what is going to happen. But if you would start to live life on your own terms, I can promise you that you will begin to experience a wonderful world you didn't think you could experience. You will find peace in knowing that you are in full control over who and what enters your life.

Understand that when you are ready to give up on your problems because they are too much to bear, God has you right where He wants you. There is no need to kill yourself because you don't see a way out. Give up on the problem, and allow God to show you the way.

I remember when I was faced with the threat of foreclosure, I booked a trip to Los Angeles, CA and did not care about spending the money irresponsibly to go out of town. I was *over it*. I booked a trip to L.A. in May 2020 for less than $200. At that time, there was a threat of murder hornets on the west coast, and I didn't even care. I didn't care about catching Coronavirus, or being stung by murder hornets, I thought my life was over and I was ready to die anyway. Do you know what happened? I gained a business idea while sitting poolside, looking up at the sky and watching the palm trees sway above me. I had given up on life, and God had me right where He wanted me. I was in a state of "Oh Well; whatever happens happens", and that's when God showed up and blessed me. Money that I was originally denied for pandemic assistance, was ultimately given to me in one large lump sum. I had the money I needed to get caught up on my mortgage, and I never foreclosed on my house. Then thee (3) months later, I didn't find a job, but a job found me. My old Vice President from a previous employer contacted me, and got me a job working at a new company he was working for making great money working 100% remotely. So see; sometimes right when you are ready to give up, you are right where God wants you to be so He can show up and show out in your life. My future seemed grim at that time, so I stopped looking towards the future and started living in the moment. You just have to hold on and be patient because things are always shifting and changing. The only thing that is constant is change.

Don't focus your attention on anything that scares you. Focus on the things you appreciate, and create an enjoyable moment in this present moment, even if that means being slightly *irresponsible* to others. Do what you need to do to create heaven on earth for the moment. Life still has its series of ups and downs for me because that's just how life works, but I give ALL of my problems I can't avoid or control to God. If someone is mad at me over how I live my life, or they have decided that they no longer like me; oh well. That's not my problem, that's theirs. If someone has a problem with you, let them keep it their problem. I don't allow others to project their problems onto me. You don't have to deal with people at all. You can just go about your life doing the things you love with those who love you.

Whatever you choose to do, do not use suicide as a method to inflict guilt on anyone. As a person who has been on both sides of the spectrum, trust me that does not work. People will miss you but eventually they will move on because that's life. Life is forever moving along and changing. A person who hurt you or mistreated you may feel bad for a short period of time, but you will be dead forever, leaving behind family and loved ones who also have to pay the price for one person's wrong doings.

In life, you have to recognize four (4) things or else you will go insane:

1. That you are always a work in progress, and life is forever showing and teaching you more about yourself. We all make mistakes, it's ok just to learn from them. Life is about the mastery of self. It may not make sense now, but in hindsight, it will.

2. Life is a direct reflection of the choices you have made thus far. No matter what, just know you have a choice. Make sure your choices align with the outcome that you truly want for yourself. Take the time to rest and disconnect from the world, and then when you are ready to re-emerge, make a choice about how you want your life to go and move in that direction. Never make a choice that could result in permanent consequences, based on temporary emotions.

3. Life is always guiding you in the right direction. You are either winning or learning. Rejection is protection, always remember that.

4. Love what and who loves you, and don't waste your energy or time on anything else. There are billions of humans on this planet. Someone that you have never met is still waiting to meet you, and they will be able to relate to you in many ways.

I would like to see you take back control of your life and create a plan on how you would like to live your life without fear. I have some questions that may help you get started.

Question for the Reader:

If you aren't afraid to die, why are you afraid to live?

_____

_____

_____

What do you think is going to happen to you if you die?

_____

_____

_____

Do you feel powerless or weak? If so, how come?

_____

_____

_____

If not, how are you willing to use your new found power to create the life you want?

_____

_____

_____

Where would you like to live?

_____

_____

_____

With whom?

_____

_____

_____

What would you like to do to earn money? How much would you like to earn?

_____

_____

_____

What types of activities are fun that you would love to do everyday if you could?

_____

_____

_____

What type of relationships would you like to have?

_____

_____

_____

What type of people would best suit your personality and give you a sense of belonging?

_____

_____

_____

Are you willing to take the necessary steps to go out and meet like minded people and do the things you love?

_____

_____

_____

Are you willing to learn new skills and reinvent yourself?

_____

_____

_____

If so, what type of skills do you need to start your journey towards becoming an expert, and who do you want to become?

_____

_____

_____

In Section IV I will provide you with resources to help you regain the hope and encouragement you need to live life more courageously, as well as find a community of like minded people who you may be able to relate to.

Section IV.
Family/Friends of Suicide Victims

Whenever we lose a loved one from suicide, the first thing we wish is that we had said or did something to prevent it. Here are some common signs of suicidal tendencies to look out for provided by NIHM.gov:

Signs and Symptoms

- Talking about wanting to die or wanting to kill themselves

- Talking about feeling empty, hopeless, or having no reason to live

- Making a plan or looking for a way to kill themselves, such as searching for lethal methods online, stockpiling pills, or buying a gun

- Talking about great guilt or shame

- Talking about feeling trapped or feeling that there are no solutions

- Feeling unbearable pain (emotional pain or physical pain)

- Talking about being a burden to others

- Using alcohol or drugs more often

- Acting anxious or agitated
- Withdrawing from family and friends
- Changing eating and/or sleeping habits
- Showing rage or talking about seeking revenge
- Taking great risks that could lead to death, such as driving extremely fast
- Talking or thinking about death often
- Displaying extreme mood swings, suddenly changing from very sad to very calm or happy
- Giving away important possessions
- Saying goodbye to friends and family
- Putting affairs in order, making a will

If these warning signs apply to you or someone you know, get help as soon as possible, particularly if the behavior is new or has increased recently.

You normally won't notice the signs because people are embarrassed to talk about their feelings or feel they don't want to be a burden on others. If you want to know what you could do to help or protect your loved one from acting on their suicidal thoughts, the answer is simple; be available, be empathetic, and listen without judgement or offering unwarranted advice. Be more curious than you are judgmental. Be more of a listener than a speaker. Listen to understand and give advice only when asked. Last but not least, never dismiss someone who says they want to commit suicide as an idol threat. Even if you feel they are *"doing it for attention'*, or *'they are just saying that as a cry for help'*, that is still no reason to write them off. It may seem a bit dramatic or unnecessary to you, but to them they are in desperate need for help. The help you can give them can be simple and require very little effort. Your presence may be all they need at that moment. Even if it's not, at least you won't feel guilty later and will know you did the best you could. Here is a list of things you can do to help according to NIMH:

1. ASK: "Are you thinking about killing yourself?" It's not an easy question, but studies show that asking at-risk individuals if they are suicidal does not increase suicides or suicidal thoughts.

2. KEEP THEM SAFE: Reducing a suicidal person's access to highly lethal items or places is an important part of suicide prevention. While this is not always easy, asking if the at-risk person has a plan and removing or disabling the lethal means can make a difference.

3. BE THERE: Listen carefully and learn what the individual is thinking and feeling. Research suggests acknowledging and talking about suicide

may reduce rather than increase suicidal thoughts.

4. HELP THEM CONNECT: Save the National Suicide Prevention Lifeline's (1-800-273-TALK (8255)) and the Crisis Text Line's number (741741) in your phone, so it's there when you need it. You can also help make a connection with a trusted individual like a family member, friend, spiritual advisor, or mental health professional.

5. STAY CONNECTED: Staying in touch after a crisis or after being discharged from care can make a difference. Studies have shown the number of suicide deaths goes down when someone follows up with the at-risk person.

No matter what happens, please do not blame yourself for the death of your loved one in the event they do commit suicide. I know that may sound harsh, but the truth is, if you could have saved them you would have, but you can't save or protect a person who has never communicated their needs to you. So many people suffer in silence and no one realizes it until it's too late. You can't help someone if you don't know they need help.

There is a difference between a person who is contemplating suicide, and a person who has already made up their mind they are going to commit suicide. The biggest and most important difference is impulsive behavior vs. overthinkers. Not everyone is fearless of death. For some people the only reason they haven't committed suicide is because they *are* afraid to die. They overthink *everything* and they are not sure what is on the other side of death. I definitely fall into the overthinker category. I just can't see myself actually going through with the act of killing myself without knowing what the end result will be. I feel more in control alive than dead. Especially knowing what I know now, and having realigned myself with my purpose.

For those individuals who are impulsive, they will need to be heavily monitored and never left alone without some form of supervision. Impulsive people are not thinking about anything, they are only acting. The threat of going to a fiery place called "hell" doesn't seem to be any better than their current state of affairs so they are willing to kill themself with the intentions of successfully accomplishing just that at any given moment. If no one can help them understand why the power of having control over their life while alive is better than having no control over their life once they're dead; I fear they will act impulsively, or without any second thought, and leave behind regret and heartbreak for so many. In those cases, if you don't catch those people in the act early enough, it will be too late to try and stop them. This is why it is important never to blame yourself if a loved one dies from suicide. It is not your fault, this was a choice that was carried out without giving it too much thought.

Once someone has made up their mind that living is more painful than anything they could possibly experience by dying, there is not much anyone can do aside from monitor and protect them from themselves until they seek professional help. Sometimes, professional help doesn't even help. My niece's mother killed herself May 2021 after having received treatment at a mental health facility. Sometimes suicide is done by a person carrying out a decision after their mind was already made up. No one could ever understand how painful life is, and sometimes there is absolutely nothing they feel is worth living for. There is no point in trying to live a life that they no longer want on any terms, not even their own. I personally have been in a place where I have had no will to live. There was nothing I could think of that I wanted to have, be, or experience, and the only thing that kept me alive was not knowing if I attempted to kill myself if it would be successful or not. But once again, because I am an overthinker, I simply did nothing and laid in bed with my phone on Do Not Disturb and played dead until the feeling eventually passed (which it always did). Unfortunately, we have to recognize that the feeling doesn't always pass for some people, and suicide is likely to happen for those who have no one to monitor and protect them from themselves, or for those who can't afford or access professional help.

This is why it is important to express to people how much you love them, once they express or show signs that they have lost their will to live. That alone *could* do wonders. Invite them to fun events, and try to keep them around you as much as possible. They may express that they want to be alone, but insist that they accompany you and get out of the house. The more they are out doing fun things with those who genuinely love them, the less time they will have to think about suicide while in isolation. The more time people with suicidal thoughts spend alone, the more likely it is to manifest into a heartbreaking reality. I literally had to force myself to get out and do fun things with fun people, and it always made me feel better.

Whatever happens, try not to blame yourself for the result of someone else's choices. If you can't be there to protect someone from suicide, be there to love on the ones they've left behind.

Question for the Reader:

List family members and/or friends who you have not seen or heard from in a while, list children who know and love you, list friends, list strangers who are polite to you, list people who you see on a regular basis, even if you don't know their name, and list strangers who you've made smile.

_____

_____

_____

_____

_____

How do you think those people would feel if they heard that you killed yourself?

_____

_____

_____

Do you think you would eventually regret killing yourself if you did it?

_____

_____

_____

Do you think these thoughts of suicide will pass if you just give it time?

_____

_____

_____

Is there anyone that you listed that you think would take the time to talk to you?_____

If not, the next section will provide you with a list of places that can help. If this book hasn't already helped talk you off the ledge, the next chapter will provide you with professional resources that can help you.

Section V.
Resources for Professional Help

If you think this book could help someone, please give this book to them, and if they want, they can give the book back to you with the questions filled out. This will help initiate communication with someone that they trust will understand what they are going through. If you are a person who has contemplated or attempted suicide, and you have read and filled this book out, please give this book to someone who you feel comfortable sharing this information with. This book can help articulate your feelings so that someone who cares about you will know where to begin when trying to give you the love and understanding you need at this time.

If you feel you do not have anyone that cares about you that you could give this book to, I am here to help you. Social Media can be both helpful and detrimental. You have to be mindful of the type of content you allow on your feed. Follow my Instagram page @organicbeautybydrea for daily motivational content on health and wellness. I also have a free video that will further elaborate on the principles of this book on my YouTube Channel DreaTheGemini. If you would like a more private one-on-one experience discussing your specific concerns with me, you can schedule an appointment on my website https://DreaTheCoach.as.me/ .

For those who battle suicidal thoughts, I would like to provide you with a list of professional resources that can help you. Legally I have to include the National Suicide Prevention number below, although I have never had good luck using this hotline myself. Things may have changed since I last used it but none-the-less:

1. National Suicide Prevention Lifeline (NSPL) 1-800-273-TALK (8255) available 24 hours a day, 7 days a week. All calls are confidential.

   We love to tell people to seek counseling or therapy without giving them affordable resources to work with. Everyone doesn't have insurance and if you are depressed over finances, not having the money to seek the help you need can be even more painful and contribute to the ultimate decision to commit suicide.

   Before I found my job I contacted my local County Health Dept that referred me to affordable and even free counseling. I highly recommend you reach out to your local health department and request free resources or sliding scale resources to provide you with the counseling you need. We live in a world where everyone is an expert and is selling some sort of course to help you start a business or become a better person. I have had some bad and good experiences. Below are some of the resources that I have personally used that I feel were worth it to help overcome my battle with depression and suicidal thoughts, even when I was in a financial bind.

*I am not getting paid to shout these resources out. This is not a paid promotion.

These are the actual resources that I have used or have been referred to use:

2. Cerebral is a mental health subscription that provides clients with ongoing, comprehensive access to online care and medication management for a monthly rate. Website www.getcerebral.com

3. My personal therapist is Nyela Malone, LCPC. She is on the high end, but well worth it. She has a network of individuals ready to assist you at Lotus Healing, LLC, and most insurance is accepted. You can contact them at 312-966-9545 or website: www.hydeparktherapist.com

4. Sara Egert is a former colleague and friend of mine that is a Yogi and Breathwork facilitator. She can help you clear out your energetic space and create an environment that helps allow messages from a higher power to infiltrate and guide your thoughts towards your true life's purpose. Contact her:

   @sara_egert on IG or https://linktr.ee/SaraEgert

5. Diana Johnson is a former colleague and friend of mine that is now my personal Financial Retirement Consultant. She has helped me conduct a plan to eliminate debt and invest in the future. Money management is extremely important to our mental health, and Diana Johnson can help you. Contact her:

IG: @dianafinancialsolutions Email: diana@ifsga.net
Website: www.ifsga.net

6. Londrelle is an amazing spirit who has meditations and relaxing music. I went to one of his meditations in Atlanta, and meeting him in person is just as magical as his online content. His Instagram Lives on Wednesday's at 8AM EST are very soothing and helpful. You can follow him on IG: @londrelle or Website: https://linktr.ee/londrelle

7. Patrice Washington was very helpful in helping me find my purpose. She has a free program that can help you tremendously if you feel your life has no purpose. You can follow her on IG: @patricewashington or Website: https://linktr.ee/seekwisdompcw

8. Nichole Sylvester's Money Miracle Meditations helped me manifest money and shift my perspective on how I view money. She has a couple of free meditations you can try. You can

follow her on IG: @nicholesylvester or Website: https://linktr.ee/nicholesylvester

I watched a lot of YouTube between 2018 – present. Here is a list of the few people that I am subscribed to that have helped me tremendously with figuring out the trajectory of my life:

- Bob Proctor
- Sadhu Guru
- Jake Ducey
- Abraham-Hicks Publications
- Joel Osteen
- Tom Bilyeu
- Rev. Ike
- T.D. Jakes
- Chloe

This is not a route that I took, but consider joining the military if you do not have a home or loved ones that care about you. The military can give you the structure, discipline, shelter, skill sets, and income to sustain yourself and help you strengthen your mind and body.

I hope this book encourages you to understand the power of your thoughts, and hopefully gives you the courage you need to live life more courageously. I hope you have a plan on how to create your own peace and heaven on earth. You are not alone in your fight to stay alive. I know that life can be painful and feel pointless at times, but life also has its fun and exciting moments which you haven't fully experienced yet. There is a group/community of people who would love to meet and support you, and could use your understanding and support as well. Always remember everything is temporary, both the good and the bad, and then one day it'll all be over. Take a deep breath, relax, and ignore any and everything that disturbs your peace until you are mentally strong enough to handle them. Go out and live life courageously, and become the best version of yourself for yourself as God intended for you to do.

www.ingramcontent.com/pod-product-compliance
Lightning Source LLC
Chambersburg PA
CBHW070210100426
42743CB00013B/3122